Jesus, the Good Shepherd
John 10:7–16 for Children

Written by Robert E. Mitchell
Illustrated by Patricia Mattozzi

ARCH® Books
Copyright © 1988 Concordia Publishing House
3558 S. Jefferson Avenue, St. Louis, MO 63118-3968
Manufactured in the United States of America

Our Savior Jesus spoke one day
To people He loved well,
"Listen to this story now
That I'm about to tell.

"Truly, this I say to you,
For sheep I am the door."
Jesus spoke of heaven, you see.
He is the only door.

"I am the way to paradise
For all, both rich and poor.
Through faith in Me you have the key
To life forevermore.

"And any other men who weren't
to be as God adored
Are only thieves and robbers, whom
My sheep are to ignore.

"The thief comes just to kill and steal;
He does not love the sheep.
All he wants to do is hurt
The poor and lowly sheep."

Jesus says to all of us,
To every girl and boy,
"I have come to give you life
That's full of peace and joy.

"I am the Shepherd of the sheep.
You understand, I pray,
That I lay down My life for you;
That dearest price I'll pay.

"For one who is a hireling
(Whose own the sheep are not)
Will see a wolf and run away.
He does not care a lot.

"The wolf will then attack the sheep
Left there so unprotected.
He snatches them and scatters them
Because they are neglected."

The wolf can be an evil man.
The sheep are you and me.
The shepherd is God's only Son,
Who died to set us free.

Then Jesus said to those who heard
"There are more sheep to find,
They need to hear their Master's ca
To all of His mankind.

"Once they learn of Me, I know
That they will heed My voice.
And when they come to Me, I know
All heaven will rejoice.

"So shall there be a shepherd—one—
And just one holy flock.
It's free to all who open wide
The door on which I knock."

Jesus is our Good Shepherd too,
For God gave Him to us.
Now we can tell the other sheep
He died upon the cross.

He died to give abundant life
To us for here and now.
And also for eternity.
In praise before Him bow!

Jesus Christ loves everyone,
There just can be no doubt.
Because I know of Jesus' love
This news I want to shout.

His sheep still hear His holy voice.
He calls, our names are heard.
And we will follow when we're called
By Jesus, the Good Shepherd.

DEAR PARENTS:

Sheep in first-century Palestine were not raised on neat farms crisscrossed by well-maintained fences. Instead, they roamed the semiarid plateaus under the watchful supervision of shepherds. At night, shepherds gathered their flocks together in pens in order to protect them from predators, both animal and human.

In John 10, Jesus confronts the Pharisees who have called Him to account for healing a blind man on the Sabbath (John 9). Jesus casts aside their legalisms: they are not the faithful shepherds of Israel. Instead they behave like thieves and robbers who seek to use the sheep of God's flock for their own purposes.

Echoing Ezek. 34:11–16, Jesus contrasts this behavior with His own: "I am the good shepherd," He affirms. "I know my sheep, and my sheep know me" (NIV).

In John 10 Jesus also pictures Himself as the gate to the sheepfold, the one way to salvation: "whoever enters [the sheepfold] through me will be saved. . . . I have come that [my sheep] may have life, and have it to the full."

Jesus tends the flock given Him by His Father because of His perfect love, and He has secured its eternal future with the ultimate sacrifice of a shepherd, His life (Rom. 5:6–8).

Rejoice with your child that the greatest Shepherd, God's Son, loves you and cares for you daily.

THE EDITOR